ADRIAN LANGENSCHEID

TRUE CRIME GERMANY

TRUE CRIMES – REAL CRIMINAL CASES

Adrian Langenscheid

TRUE CRIME GERMANY

TRUE CRIMES – REAL CRIMINAL CASES

About this book:

Cold blooded murders, a tragic kidnapping and a spectacular robbery – fifteen True Crime short stories about true, real-life German crime cases. Not even judges, prosecutors and defence lawyers are left untouched when defendants stand trial for particularly cruel acts and the shocking fates of the victims and their families are gradually revealed. In the ideal case the final judgement ensures the just punishment of the perpetrators. – In the ideal case.

About the author:

Adrian Langenscheid is a teacher, musician and educational film producer. His work, stretching across several disciplines, is largely dedicated to the narrative of human experience and the meaning of life. As a musician he received several Independence Awards. His pedagogical work has been honoured with various educational prizes. This passionate True Crime debut is released on Amazon. Together

with his wife and children Adrian lives in Stuttgart,
Baden-Wuerttemberg.

Author: Adrian Langenscheid
ISBN: 9781688877962

1st edition June 2019
© 2019 Stefan Waidelich Dachenhäuserweg 44.71101 Schönaich
Printing house: Amazon Media EU S.á r.l., 5 Rue Plaetis, L-2338, Luxembourg
Cover art: © Canva
Cover design: Pixa Heros Stuttgart

CONTENT

INTRODUCTION

Do you count yourself among the innumerable passionate fans of crime thrillers? Do you enjoy being thrilled and guessing who the perpetrator is, even before the end of an exciting book or film?

Real life writes the most interesting, touching but also the most shocking stories. What happens outside our very own front door can be absolutely incomprehensible and deeply upsetting.

In this book, we present you 15 criminal cases that actually happened, not so long ago and perhaps even in your immediate surroundings.

We present you the true, brutal facts. We only changed the names of the persons involved.

The people involved in these crimes above all have to deal with strong emotions which for instance drive the perpetrators to commit their crimes. These crimes can make the world collapse on the victims and for all those close to them.

Is it really true that most crimes are committed

out of passion? Is it true that, under certain circumstances, each of us is capable of killing another human being?

Would it have been possible to prevent some of these crimes in advance?

By reading the following stories you can find out for yourself.

Prepare to be thrilled by thirteen cruel but completely different murders, a spectacular kidnapping and a sensational theft that will inspire you to guess who the perpetrator is, and that will move you to tears!

Sense the almost unimaginable pain of the victims and their relatives! Feel the screaming injustice if the perpetrator cannot be identified in some cases or if he gets off unscathed in the end! Enjoy an extraordinary theft that is unforgotten even to this day! Put yourself in the position of those involved and marvel at how reality can overshadow even the most creative imagination!

As you read these stories, you will laugh and cry, you will be amazed, horrified and left speechless.

CHAPTER 1:
A Double Murder Without Clearly Recognizable Motives

It is one of the first spring days of the year when a neighbour knocks on the door of the nine-year-old Stefan's family.

His private surroundings know this bright boy as an enthusiastic football fan. Above all, people appreciate his friendliness and helpfulness.

Because he wasn't feeling well in the morning, Stefan didn't attend school that day. So he immediately agrees to help the 19-year-old neighbour holding the ladder for the scheduled work in his house.

By now, Stefan is fortunately feeling better again. With a quick, cheerful wave he says goodbye to his mother. At this time, nobody suspects this would be a farewell forever. Still, Stefan never comes back home afterwards.

After several hours have passed and the evening is approaching, the nine-year-old's family starts to look everywhere for him. They of course ring the bell of the neighbour he went with. But nobody answers.

Slowly, the family's initial nervousness is turning

into ever-increasing worry. Where could Stefan be? So far he has never stayed away so long without giving notice to his parents. Nobody seems to have seen him in the neighbourhood in the last few hours.

Sensing a bad omen, the family desperately circles the quiet, dark neighbour's house. When the boy's stepfather notices the open patio door, nothing holds him back. In extreme exceptional situations like this, the usual rules of conduct lose any validity.

Inside the house the family members split up. Searching the house, they keep calling Stefan's name.

Finally, the elder son of the family descends down to the basement. Shortly afterwards, he screams in panic: "Come here! Hurry! There's blood all over the place. Stefan's dying."

One of the neighbours who followed the events from outside also storms down into the cellar and immediately tries to revive the boy. Unfortunately, none of his efforts show the slightest success.

According to the emergency doctor's assessment later, Stefan had actually been dead for more than an hour by that time. The boy, dressed only in his underpants, thanks to countless stab wounds in his abdominal region.

When they find the corpse of their child, the world of the entire family is turning upside down. Even the paramedics called to the murder scene can no longer hold back their tears at the sight of the murdered boy. The almost apathetic stepfather of the nine-year-old begs them to save his boy. The mother is weeping bitterly and is calling for her child again and again.

Right from the start, the investigators inevitably suspect the 19-year-old neighbour in whose house the body was discovered. However, since his appearance at the victim's family, there has been no trace of him.

The search for the unemployed murder suspect is initiated immediately. In the course of this, the investigators search a grammar school and a hospital near the crime scene. At the same time, flyers with a detailed description of the suspect are distributed. Subsequently, within three days, the police receive more than 1,400 tips from the population.

Also, the stepfather of the murdered boy, whose circle of friends includes the members of a well-known rocker group, announces that they would be on the look for the perpetrator.

In order to prevent imminent vigilante justice, the police storm the Rocker Group's clubhouse the following evening. However, they are unable prove that it has any serious intentions in this respect.

On the evening of the third day of the search, the suspect, whose left hand is injured, turns himself in to the police in a snack bar. He informs the officials about a house fire in the neighbourhood.

After having extinguished the fire, the fire department calls in the investigators. In the burnt-out apartment they find another male victim, killed again by several stab wounds. This is the 22-year-old acquaintance of the suspect, who gave him shelter following the first murder.

As a result, the suspect confesses and describes the two murders in completely cold and uninvolved manner. As the possible trigger for his acts, he's only able to state his disappointment at the rejection of his application to the German army. He doesn't give any further reasons.

Only now the investigators receive final proof of how closely these two murders are interconnected. However, when looking for a motive and an explanation, they are still in the dark. All throughout his interrogations, the suspect remains shockingly cold and emotionless.

He had even bragged about the crime on the Internet, with several photos of his first, nine-year-old murder victim. Equally incomprehensible is the fact that one of his acquaintances spread these pictures via WhatsApp. Following that, other users who had seen these pictures asked him to inform the police.

Why didn't he come up with the idea himself? What led him to spread these horrible images?

Because they were on an American server, the photos could not even be deleted to spare the victim's family the additional pain.

These two senseless murders caused a stir throughout Germany and in neighbouring countries, and shocked everyone who followed the reports.

More than 800 people attended the memorial service for the two murder victims. Since the church offers space for a maximum of 500 people, the remaining 300 mourners followed the ceremony outside the church, which was transmitted over loudspeakers.

For the burial of the nine-year-old victim, the city issued a special permit for a funeral in a cemetery where no funerals had been held for years. Around 1,000 mourners appeared here, including several rocker groups, being friends with the boy's stepfather.

A few days later, more than 600 mourners attended the funeral of the 22-year-old murder victim.

Half a year later, the main trial against Matthias N. was opened. The brother and stepfather of the nine-year-old murder victim were unable to cope with this enormous emotional strain and were unable to testify as witnesses. The parents of the alleged perpetrator exercised their right to refuse to give evidence.

In January of the following year, Matthias N. was sentenced according to adult criminal law by the regional court, based on the clear and conclusive results of the investigation. Because of the double murder and the particular severity of his guilt, the offender must serve a life sentence.

Altogether he had inflicted more than 120 stab wounds on his two victims. He himself did not comment on his actions in court.

The expert appointed by the court described the personality of the murderer as psychopathic, sadistic and narcissistic.

Trial observers found the testimony of the perpetrator's sister even more shocking. She was clearly under strong pressure, but felt obliged to answer all questions truthfully, even despite her right to refuse to give evidence. She said she owed this to the mothers of the two victims. She had also been very fond of the nine-year-old son of her former neighbours and had firmly believed that he could one day become something very special.

Among other things, she explained that her brother had been violent, emotionally cold, indifferent and lonely all his life. After threatening his first-grade teacher with scissors, he was in therapy for the first time at the age of seven or eight. She too would have been afraid of him from an early age and warned her friends about him. She would never have seen her brother as proudly before as she saw him after the two murders.

The perpetrator's sister ended her statement with the poignant words that they had once been siblings, but that she wanted nothing more to do with the boy sitting in front of her.

Would everything perhaps have been different if the perpetrator's conspicuous behaviour and tendency to violence had been taken seriously early on? And would his two victims still be alive today in that case?

CHAPTER 2:
Murder in the Penthouse

In May 2006 it is already pleasantly warm and sunny in Southern Germany. Even in the big cities the increasing feel of anticipation of the approaching summer is palpable.

All around nature is greening and blossoming. The beer gardens are well-patronized and locals as well as tourists enjoy the warm evenings in the fresh air. At this time of year, the almost Mediterranean flair of the city unmistakeably awakens.

59-year-old Clara B., single since the death of her husband and exceedingly wealthy, is one of the few locals not to be infected by the spring fever. The weather cannot change her regular daily routine.

All her life, she has been extremely disciplined and holding her purse. Now she finally wallows in the luxury she dreamed of as a child in her home in Eastern Europe.

This luxury includes her tastefully furnished penthouse apartment in one of the city's posh districts.

Here she feels comfortable and secure. Even though she has been a widow for eleven years, she is by no means lonely.

Her friends and their established routines play a vital role in her strictly planned everyday life. Those closer to her above all appreciate her honesty and reliability.

On a mild early summer evening, Clara B. reaches for her handbag to leave her apartment. Like every Monday night, it's time for her regulars' table. She intends to appear there on time as she always does.

What most likely happened after she opened her apartment door is based on the findings of investigations that take place later.

A man dressed in black is waiting for her outside the door. In the darkness of the stairwell he practically merges into the wall. Since this man is familiar with her routines, he knows that Clara B. leaves her apartment every Monday at exactly the same time. Everything points to the fact that he specifically chose this time..

Before Clara B. can even set a foot outside, the man pushes her back into her apartment. Without saying a single word, he immediately begins to hit her with a hard, heavy object.

Clara B. is hit on the head by a total of 24 brutal blows.

The following day, her body is discovered at the foot of a spiral staircase in her apartment. Did she perhaps try to escape up these stairs immediately before her death? Did she still have sufficient strength for that?

The autopsy of the victim reveals that Clara B. was probably beaten to death with a hammer or a similar tool. According to the forensic expert, the blows caused severe bleeding, central paralysis and severe craniocerebral injury.

The victim's head shows traces of black paint. However, the murder weapon is never found.

The investigators soon suspect the nephew of the murdered woman, who was present when the body was found. In their opinion, no one but him seriously qualifies as a suspect.

They assume pure greed as the motive. He allegedly killed his aunt to secure his inheritance ahead of time. This assumption is affirmed by the fact that Klaus K., the victim's nephew, had just abandoned his studies. Was he afraid his aunt would soon cut off his money due to this?

In the course of the interrogations, Klaus K. protests his innocence again and again.

According to his statement, he was lying down in the bed with a severe cold on the day of the murder. Because there are no witnesses for this, he is unable to produce an alibi.

On the victim's clothes and on the envelope of the testament, the investigators secure DNA traces that can be attributed to Klaus K. The defence considers this evidence meaningless because the suspect frequently entered and left his aunt's apartment. So he might have left his DNA there at an earlier date as well.

In the suspect's purse, investigators find several 500 Euro notes with DNA traces of his aunt and tiny blood particles. The forensic scientist is unable to determine with whose blood this is exactly.

Finally, the defence requests a 3D reconstruction of the murder scene. The main aim is to clarify whether the perpetrator was left-handed or right-handed. The investigations have shown that the murderer is most likely to be right-handed. Initially, this speaks for the left-handed Klaus K., but even the simulation of the chain of events does not bring any final clarity, as a left-handed person with the corresponding weapon in his right hand can strike just as hard.

The case becomes even more mysterious when DNA traces are secured in the victim's penthouse that resemble DNA from the scene of another murder. However, as these are contaminated, the court is not allowing them as evidence later.

In May 2007, the main trial against Klaus K. begins, lasting 15 months with more than 90 trial days. Finally, the circumstantial evidence, the suspected motive, the lack of an alibi and the behaviour of the accused following the murder are enough for the court to sentence him to life imprisonment.

Additionally, he is accused of having stolen more than 3,500 Euro from his aunt the year before the crime, confirming the presumed motive of greed. Also, his studies, that he had discontinued directly prior to the crime and of which Clara B. was unaware, as well as the long years of humiliation by his aunt seem to underline his guilt. According to several testimonies, she used every opportunity to lesson him and control his life. She allegedly even wanted to have a say in the choice of his girlfriend. Nevertheless, the defence still insists that Klaus K. is innocent.

On the day of the crime, for example, the defendant supposedly came to the scene of the crime by bicycle, which he cleaned that same evening in the multi-storey car park with a high-pressure cleaner. Would he really have removed the possibly existing traces of blood in public? His defence attorney believes that no one with an at least reasonably clear mind would do that.

Furthermore considerable is the well-known fact that Clara B. had no confidence in the banks and therefore constantly stored exceptionally high amounts of cash in her apartment. Several witnesses claim that she partly kept it in plastic bags. At the crime scene in the victim's penthouse, numerous drawers and cupboards were found torn open. Only the safe was still locked.

Can a robbery murder be assumed if nobody knows how much money was in the apartment and if anything was stolen at all?

Some witnesses brought up the mysterious coincidence that one of the murder victim's friends was in permanent financial trouble. After the crime, according to their statements, he suddenly would have appeared relieved from his money worries.

A so-called insider even considers a murder conspiracy, involving several friends of the murdered woman, as possible.

Yet, there's no evidence to prove this. In consequence, the court is unimpressed by this and the verdict is made final.

The defence appeals against the judgement, but the Federal Supreme Court confirms the original court decision.

Under normal circumstances, Klaus K. would have been granted exactly half of the victim's estate. The court declares this inheritance share "forfeited" due to the verdict. Half of Clara B.'s assets would thus go to the state.

In spring 2011, Klaus K.'s brother files a lawsuit against the convicted in a civil lawsuit for inequitable inheritance. His intention however, is not to do him harm. Instead, he wants to prevent the state from receiving half of the inheritance and to force the judiciary to open another evidence procedure.

After all, Klaus K.'s entire family continues to stand behind him and firmly believes in his innocence. Following the conviction, it even offered a reward of 250,000 Euro for new relevant information leading to the conviction of the real offender.

As Klaus K. is unwilling to defend himself against his brother's civil lawsuit, his brother is ultimately awarded the entire inheritance and the state comes out empty-handed.

A little while later, a group of supporters of Klaus K. calls for a retrial. This application is dismissed by the district court and subsequently by the higher

regional court.
Klaus K. will remain in prison at least until 2028.
In February 2019, he again applied to the regional court for the trial to be reopened.
At every opportunity, he affirms his innocence with the same sentence: "I have a clear conscience."

CHAPTER 3:
Shots in the Woods

For many years now, the High Consistory member Richard A. has lived with his wife Regina and their two almost grown up children in a pretty house on the edge of the woods. All in all, the happy family is popular with their neighbours. Richard A., very busy and responsible for the Evangelical Lutheran Church and a member of the Synod of German Evangelical Churches, has little time to spare. As soon as one of the rare opportunities presents itself, the nature lover regains his strength riding and hunting. For this reason he leased a nearby piece of forest a while ago.

The spouses like to call this forest their own small piece of the paradise, a place to relax from the hustle and bustle of everyday life and find peace and quiet.

Their regular habits include walks in the forest with their hunting dogs, even in wind and weather. And as they enjoy them so much, they usually take a little longer on Sundays.

Even on this wet and cold, gloomy Sunday morning in February 1997, which will change the life of the family forever, they look forward to their beloved walk in the forest.

At this time, their daughter is already living and studying in another federal state. Their younger brother, who attends Grammar School and is just about to graduate, still lives with his parents.

Even on Sundays, the family is up and about early. It has been their custom for years to talk about the most important events of the past week while having breakfast together.

As always, the family dog quickly becomes restless and feels drawn to his personal hunting ground outside. So, the parents soon say goodbye to their son, who has to learn at home for an upcoming exam.

Everything can be reconstructed up to this point. The following things happening in the woods, however, are based exclusively on the results of later investigations.

Most likely, the spouses out of the blue hear shots during their walk. Since Richard A. feels responsible for his piece of the forest, he immediately decides to get to the bottom of the matter. Is somebody organizing illegal shooting exercises here?

The tenant will not allow this under any circumstances. To find out what's going on, the two of them diverge from their path without hesitation. Step by step through the dense undergrowth, they approach the shots' point of origin.

A moment after, they step out into a small clearing right in front of one or perhaps several shooters who by no chance were reckoning with someone discovering their actions that deep in the woods by pure chance.

Most definitely, Richard A. dauntlessly asks the shooter or shooters to stop shooting immediately. Probably in the same breath, he threatens to report them to the police.

This first leads to a verbal confrontation between the shooter, or shooters, and the unwelcome witnesses.

Within seconds, the situation escalates. As Richard A. refuses to be intimidated by threats, the spouses and its dog suddenly become the target.

Probably mainly out of fear of being reported to the police, the perpetrator, or perpetrators, fire several targeted pistol shots at the married couple and the dog.

Richard A. is killed by two shots in the head and two in the abdomen, his wife by two shots in the head. Their loyal hunting dog, too, dies from his severe gunshot wounds, still at the scene of the crime. Certainly he was trying to defend his master and mistress.

Since there were no other people near the crime scene at that time, the perpetrator, or perpetrators, manage to escape unseen. They leave their victims in the clearing, shot dead at close range.

Around 1:00 PM two walkers from a neighbouring village discover the bodies of the two and the dog in the forest.

The police find numerous shells and cartridge cases at the crime scene. Even a signpost has been hit by shots several times. The two pistols matching the cartridge cases had been stolen from a lawyer's office by unknown persons a few weeks earlier. This theft has been reported properly.

The public is extremely shocked and takes an active interest in the fate of the two murder victims. An evidence of this fact is, among other things, the large number of mourners attending the memorial service and the burial of the couple by the regional bishop at that time.

The police offer a high reward for relevant information leading to the arrest of the perpetrators. However, despite the extensive investigations into the circumstances of the crime, not until four years later, the investigators succeed in proving the involvement of a suspect, at this time 34-year-old, in this crime. The suspect is convicted as a result of the analysis of DNA samples, as a cigarette butt found at the crime scene undoubtedly belonged to him. Up to this point, the suspect was known to the police as a burglar. Because of his involvement in a robbery his DNA had already been entered into the database six years prior to the murders.

The suspect confesses the crime immediately after his arrest, but he later revokes his confession and increasingly starts to contradict himself.

Despite the still uncertain points, the trial against the accused is opened in January 2001. During the trial, the accused admits that he stole the weapons from the lawyer's office and witnessed the double murder. He names two men from the drug milieu of a nearby city as the actual perpetrators.

The evidence remains incomplete until the end and the exact circumstances of the crime cannot be reconstructed. Even the issue of who actually fired the weapon cannot be answered with absolute certainty. In addition, there are rumours that the double murder might have been a late revenge of the former Stasi.

Richard A., who in the former GDR was described by the Stasi as a "hostile pastor", actually had been involved in reviewing the Stasi documents after the fall of the Berlin Wall.

Nevertheless, the court considers the original confession of the accused in the presence of several persons to be credible. During the course of this confession, the accused had shown unmistakable regret and even cried.

Finally, the judge concludes that the defendant's guilt has been proven sufficiently. He would have made an impulsive decision in a split second that lead to the death of two people. At the same time, the perpetrator destroyed his own life with this.

When the defendant is found guilty and sentenced to life imprisonment in June 2001, his defender is shocked. He announces his intention to appeal against the verdict in any case, especially because of the hitherto unknown, suspected accomplices. The defendant himself seems almost uninvolved throughout the entire trial.

This purely by impulse-driven murder, the verdict of the court, as well as the remaining doubts about the convicted being guilty stir the hearts of the people to this day – and certainly all the more since the convicted, after 15 years, was released from custody in spring 2015. Until the end of the set probation period in January 2020, he is under supervision at his place of residence.

Is he really the killer? Did he commit the crime alone, or did he just protect his accomplices?

What do the relatives of the murder victims feel at the thought of him now being a free man again?

This crime likewise has changed the lives of the bereaved from the bottom up, as illustrated by the life of the killed couple's son.

Prior to the murder of his parents, the young man had never intended to follow in his father's footsteps. Since his parents had brought him and his sister up Christian but in spiritual freedom, he had been determined to follow his own path.

It was the sudden death of his parents that finally moved him to become a priest after all. He justifies this move with the fact that his faith in the most difficult time after the tragic loss had been everything he was able hold on to.

He holds no hatred for the convicted. Instead, he is convinced that the true perpetrator or perpetrators now have to live with what they did to his parents.

Many of the open questions regarding this crime will probably never be answered satisfyingly.

A foundling in the forest in the east of the country reminds us of this mysterious criminal case to this day. The stone is engraved with the names of the two murder victims, who will remain unforgotten far beyond the borders of their home.

CHAPTER 4:

A Voice from the Past

Together with her four siblings, the strikingly pretty, dark-haired Renate R. grows up in one of western Germany's rural regions. Her parents, Germans expelled from Silesia at a young age, do not actually live in prosperity, but they are fairly satisfied with what they have. They lovingly raise their children to be happy even in humble conditions.

Most people associate a residence in the country with the romantic idea of finding inner peace and quiet in harmony with nature. But living in the countryside also has its downsides.

Throughout her life, Renate R.'s parents worked hard and had to make many sacrifices. For them, everything is about their children. Their greatest desire is to smooth their way to a better future.

Despite all her efforts and her eagerness to learn, Renate R. does not find an apprenticeship or a job in her local area after graduating from school. This leaves her very sad as she wants to support her family and achieve something in life.

In the summer of 1981, shortly before her seventeenth birthday, she meets Hubert M., three years older and son of a wealthy farmer from a nearby village. For Renate R. it is love at first sight. The modest young woman is in seventh heaven and dreams of a future together with the man she thinks is the love of her life.

Since the young man grew up in a completely different social situation, her parents become increasingly worried. Still, they don't have the heart to hurt their daughter's feelings and destroy her dreams.

Hubert M.'s parents have their own completely different reasons for mistrusting their son's budding relationship with Renate R. In their book, their son deserves someone much better and they are afraid the young woman might only be after his money.

Again and again they take their son to task and warn him not to make a serious mistake that would ruin his life.

Because of their constant accusations and their ongoing criticism of his romance with Renate R., Hubert M. gives his girlfriend the sack after one year.

A little later he hears that Renate R. is pregnant from him and that, in her desperation after the split-up, she attempted suicide. Tormented by remorse, he gets into contact with her again. The two of them have a talk and Hubert M. suggests that they should remain friends in the future.

A few weeks later Renate R. finds a job as a seamstress in one of the nearby towns. There she moves into a small flat to stand by her own from now on.

On a cold, rain-swept November evening, the neighbours hear a violent argument in this flat. In the course of this, Renate R. tries to force Hubert M. to marry her because of her pregnancy. However, he firmly rejects this idea.

Instead, he asks her to come to his father's farm the following day. He would like to make a proposal to the young woman to settle the whole matter with a financial compensation. He is hoping for a definitive solution to get rid of the unwanted invader in his family forever.

The next day at noon, Renate R. is seen for the last time, when a co-worker gives her a ride in her car. Renate R. asked her for this favour to arrive at the family farm on time for the appointment with Hubert M. and his father. Renate R. leaves the car near the farm and says goodbye to her colleague. She explains to her that she prefers to walk the rest of the way on foot.

At this point, Renate R. disappears without leaving a single further trace. A few days later her family, which has not heard from her since, files a missing person's report.

In the course of the investigation, the police raise multiple theories regarding the cause of Renate R.'s disappearance. Since the draft for a suicide note was found in her flat, investigators are considering a second suicide attempt, among other things. However, the fact that the body of the young woman is nowhere to be found speaks against this.

Also, there are rumours that Renate R. has indicated the intent to disappear and start a new life in another place.

Despite these suspicions, with every day passing without a trace of the missing person, Hubert M., the father of her unborn child, is increasingly falling under suspicion. During the interrogations, however, he asserts that Renate R. had left the farm completely unharmed on foot, following the conversation with his father.

Since there is no evidence for this fact and Renate R. remains missing, the investigations finally lead to nothing.

In February of the following year, about ten kilometres from the place where Renate R. was seen last, some teen walkers discover a bunch of keys in a cemetery. Her family identifies these as the property of her missing daughter.

Although this remains the last hint, the file is never closed. With criminal offences such as this, this is the normal course of action.

Not until 29 years later, in the summer of 2011, a well-known television programme reminds it's viewers of Renate R.'s disappearance. After such a long time without any new findings, investigators assume the young woman was killed and her body removed. Renate R.'s mother, who has grown very old by that time, is still tormented day after day by the uncertainty about the her daughter's fate.

The host of the programme describes the events of this time and, above all, appeals to the consciences of possible accomplices., because their joint guilt would have been time-barred by now.

Even before the end of the television programme, a female witness comes forward with crucial information about a male person involved in the crime almost three decades ago, a close friend of Hubert M.

During his interrogation the accomplice finally breaks down and confesses that, back then, he helped his friend Hubert M. removing the body of Renate R.

As a result of this statement, the now 50-year-old Hubert M. is taken into custody in September 2011. On the basis of the information provided by the accomplice, the police are intensively searching for the corpse of Renate R. for two weeks. In October 2011, they find a human skeleton at a landfill that has been closed down for several years. The skeleton is wrapped in plastic foil together with the remains of women's clothing.

Only a few days later, the results of the DNA tests carried out by forensic physicists provide final confirmation. The skeleton represents the mortal remains of Renate R.

At the beginning of November 2011, she finds her last rest next to her father's grave, together with her unborn child.

Two days before New Year's Eve, the public prosecutor's office initiates proceedings against Hubert M. for murder. The trial begins in March 2012. The defendant remains silent from the first to the last day of the trial.

One of the main witnesses is the former landlord of the victim, who is able to reproduce the bitter dispute between Renate R. and her later murderer almost word for word.

For the prosecutor, the results of the investigation and the testimony with absolute certainty lead to the following verdict: The day after their heated argument, Renate R. appeared at the agreed time on the farm of Hubert M's father. However, a financial settlement was not enough for her. Instead, she tried once more to change the mind of her unborn child's father and to persuade him to marry her.

As a result, the defendant decided to strangle his girlfriend and then bury her body at a nearby landfill.

The court, too, is convinced of the correctness of these assumptions and of Hubert M.'s guilt. In June 2012, however, the defendant is nevertheless acquitted.

As a reason for its decision, the court states that after almost thirty years, the victim's remains provided no clear evidence of murder. From a legal point of view, the court therefore had to assume the criminal offence of manslaughter which became time-barred after twenty years.

The Chief Prosecutor calls this judgement an unsatisfactory result. Due to the current legal situation,

however, the court would be forced to accept it. It will examine though whether an appeal might be worthwhile.
This trial leaves an exceptionally uncomfortable feeling in everyone involved.
A voice from the past was heard begging for justice. However, its pleas remained unanswered.

CHAPTER 5:
Crumb Gate

It is vital for the survival of any company to market and sell its products in a way that promises as much success as possible. Amongst other things, creative mascots and company logos with a high recognition value play a decisive role here.

This inspires one of the most famous and traditional pastry manufacturers in our country to attach a golden cookie to the façade of its company headquarters.

This is a replica of the company's popular Leibniz cookie, weighting about twenty kilograms, made of brass and then gilded. Bahlsen commissioned a renowned sculptor to design this gem for its company building.

In 2006, it's finally happening. From now on, the golden cookie on the façade of the company building shines, competing with the sun and marvelled at by pedestrians.

But on a gloomy, wet and cold morning at the beginning of 2013, this precious piece of work disappears all of a sudden.

The first employees who hurry into their offices on this day stand puzzled in front of the building that suddenly seems so unusually bare and dull. Who in the world comes up with the idea of stealing such a heavy brass cookie that you can't even eat? What are the thieves planning to do with it?

Basically, the cookie only has real value for the company itself; no one will buy it, that's for sure. After all, it would immediately attract attention on any other building and certainly the oversized pastry is unsuitable as interior decoration.

Shortly after the stealthy heist, the company and the editorial team of one of the largest newspapers in the northern German state receive a blackmailing letter. Enclosed with this letter is a photograph showing a stranger in a cookie monster costume in front of the golden cookie.

In their letter, the blackmailers demand the pastry manufacturer to donate a certain amount of chocolate cookies to a children's hospital and transfer 1,000 Euro to an animal shelter.

If their demands are not met, the blackmailers threaten to dispose of the golden cookie at a landfill, putting a terrible end to its life.

The company's management calls a press conference and announces it will under no circumstances respond to the blackmailers' demands. Instead, it agrees to donate more than 50,000 packs of its popular cookie to 52 welfare institutions after the voluntary return of the stolen cookie.

In their following letter, the blackmailers accept this proposal of the company management.

Already on the following day, the golden cookie is back again out of the blue. Attached by a red bow, it hangs on a well-known monument in front of the city university building.

Although it is easy to prove that this is indeed the original, the investigations against the unknown thieves and blackmailers continue at full speed.

The state office of criminal investigation immediately examines the returned cookie for fingerprints, for DNA and fibre traces.

But the blackmailers, too, don't remain idle. Two days later, a third letter from the cookie hijackers arrives. They demand that the company management's promise is to be kept. The management affirms its commitment and asks local non-profit institutions to apply for one of the previously announced cookie donations.

Shortly thereafter, a television programme rekindles the interest in the kidnapping of the golden cookie with a small sensation. In an anonymous interview, four unknown persons, three men and one woman, confess the spectacular crime. Their identity, however, remains a secret.

On the day following the broadcast of that programme, the company publishes the names of the recipients of the cookie donations, which were selected by lot. Immediately afterwards, the first deliveries are on their way.

In the meantime, the department of public prosecution has converted the investigations of extortion and theft into a case of property damage. After all, the cookie has reappeared.

As the identity of the perpetrators remains unknown despite all efforts, the process is finally closed in May 2013.

Whether the cookie thieves are actually guilty of an offence within the meaning of the applicable law remains controversial in legal circles.

At the national and international level, however, this puzzling crime attracts a great deal of attention. The cookie manufacturer, of course, also benefits from this.

The cookie manufacturer would have had to invest about 1.7 million Euro for advertisements to generate a similar response. Compared to this sum, the company did not even spend 40,000 Euro for delivering the donation packages.

These considerations here and there lead to speculations that the heist might have been a particularly imaginative marketing strategy. However, there is no evidence to prove this, and the company management strongly denies any presumed involvement in the crime.

According to the management, it under no circumstances would have risked criminal liability just for advertising purposes. This statement is supported by the fact that the cookie manufacturer had reported the theft and extortion to the police on the day of the mysterious disappearance of its unique gem.

Additionally, the company points out that under no circumstances would it have accepted the risk of inspiring and encouraging potential imitators.

In connection to the considerations about advertising effectiveness of the cookie heist there were reports about a well-known advertising agency that published large-scale announcements in several newspapers just before the day of the return of the unusual stolen property. In these it offered the cookie thieves jobs as PR consultants.

One of our country's leading criminologists has a different angle on this tricky matter. He assumes that there is a bet or a very special test of courage behind this extraordinary crime.

This unprecedented criminal case moves the people, but the vast majority of the population looks at all that with humour. Even the popular television programme Sesame Street gives an amusing commentary on the events. In it, the worldwide popular cookie monster swears: "me no steal the golden cookie", it had nothing to do with the theft of the golden cookie.

As spring 2013 draws to a close, things have gradually calmed down and the adventurous pastry is preparing for another big appearance. Now the returned and meanwhile newly polished golden cookie shines for four weeks while displayed in an exhibition in the State Museum.

The inventor of the much smaller but edible twin of

the former abduction victim makes amusing comments at the opening of the exhibition, as does the artist who created the cookie.

Curious museum visitors stream in vast numbers to the front of the now Germany-wide famous cookie, which went through so much more than any other piece of pastry. A new star is born.

Only in July 2013 the golden cookie is able to recover from its strains. Freshly restored and even brighter than ever before, it finally returns to its original place. Here it can breathe a sigh of relief. In particular as its owners have ensured that it is save from similar adventures in the future. From now on it will be technically monitored on the façade of the company building.

In the course of the following months, various television shows make sure its sudden fame doesn't fade too quickly. Several scriptwriters are all too happy to use the story of the cookie that travelled so far as an inspiration.

To this day, the identity of the cookie thieves remains a mystery. But their bold deed will be remembered for a long time to come. And in the end, their names don't play the slightest role.

For some years now, the golden cookie has been hanging again where it belongs. Perhaps it sometimes smiles at the thought of how much joy its edible relatives have given to the recipients of the cookie donations.

CHAPTER 6:
Helpfulness With Serious Consequences

In the central part of our country, Karl and Maria S. live in a spacious, cosily furnished villa on the slope of a mountain.

The wealthy industrial couple can look back on a strenuous life with countless ups and downs, in which it wasn't spared from strokes of fate.

The two of them honestly deserve being able to fulfil their dream of finding peace and quiet in nature, far away from the next village.

At that time, 1937 seems to belong almost to another age. Back then, Karl S.'s father applied for a patent for a hand-operated kitchen appliance for stirring and beating that he had already presented the year before at the Leipziger Mustermesse. Following this, he manufactured his invention at home, with the active support of his family. As demand grew steadily, he soon found himself forced to rent factory premises. Thus, a young, ambitious company saw the light of day.

The first severe setback soon followed when the Second World War broke out. As the required materials could no longer be procured, production had to be discontinued.

In October 1943 the family home was destroyed in a bombing raid. Together with their children Karl and Petra, the parents found temporary shelter in a monastery.

After the end of the war, Karl S.'s father immediately rebuilt his company to be able to produce his popular kitchen appliance and universal machine tools again as quickly as possible. Until its progressive replacement by electrically operated appliances in the 1970s, his kitchen machine was essential in almost every German household. In total, about eight million of the popular devices had been produced by 1997.

During the company's heyday years, Karl S. joined at a young age, in order to relieve his father and take over the business after the retirement of the company founder.

In order to fulfil their heart's desire and to share their wealth, the professionally successful married couple Karl and Maria S. adopted two girls, Kathrin and Sabine S.

So much for the history of the family. Now let's return to the year 1997 and to the villa!

On a pleasantly mild evening in June 1997, the couple S. made themselves comfortable in their home in the forest. The two sit together after an early dinner in the living room, Maria S. reads an exciting book and Karl S. is busy with the daily mail. Their two adopted daughters are constantly out and about and again not with them this evening.

The fact that their villa is located far away from the other houses does not trouble the married couple. They rely on their home being well secured by an alarm system and several surveillance cameras.

Dawn is approaching, when the doorbell rings. Since they're not expecting any visitors, the two of them look at each other questioning. Then Karl S. answers the door. In front of him he finds a young couple he has never met before: Felix L., who is 24 at the time, and his 19-year-old girlfriend Helga A., who is 24 at that time.

The two politely apologize for the disturbance and ask Karl S. for making a call from his house as their car broke down. Karl S. lets them in readily. Helping others in difficult situations is something natural for him.

Immediately after the fake phone call, Felix L. out of the blue goes for the landlord and slits his throat with a knife from his trouser pocket. Karl S. goes down and is dead within a few seconds.

The later results of the investigation lead to the assumption that Maria S., despite being in shock, still attempted to escape the murderer. Right before the front door, however, Felix L. is catching up on her and kills her the same way as he did with her husband shortly before.

Before the two perpetrators flee into the darkness of the night, they ravage the entire house of the S.

family, rummaging through all the cupboards and drawers. However, they only do this to pretend a robbery.

Over the course of the following days, friends and acquaintances of Karl and Maria S. notice that they no longer answer the phone. Even in the nearby town, where they usually shop regularly, people begin to miss the likeable couple.

Acquaintances, which finally pay them a visit to inquire about their condition, finally discover the two murder victims.

The police officers, who are the first to arrive at the crime scene, await a horrible sight. The whole scenario immediately reminds them of a targeted execution.

In the course of the investigation, the couple's two adoptive daughters of are also questioned of course. Kathrin and Sabine S. are completely shocked and right from the start suspect that only the Russian Mafia could be responsible for such a crime and that the double murder had a business background.

At the time of the crime, Kathrin S. spent a weekend together with her fiancé Robert D. in the Allgäu, while Sabine S. stayed with a friend. Since this friend and the owner of the hotel, in which Kathrin S. had spent the night with her fiancé, confirm their alibis, the two adopted daughters don't seem suspicious at first sight.

Soon after, however, several witnesses come forward and shed a completely new light on the case. According to the witnesses' testimonies, before the murder, Sabine S. announced at school that something would happen to her parents in the near future. At about the same time, Robert D., who works as a cook for the German army, told his comrades that his parents-in-law were to be killed.

When the investigators learn that the two adoptive daughters had made an unsuccessful attempt to kill their parents with rat poison in a cake some time ago, the investigation arrives at a critical turning point. The parents only survived this assassination because they did not want to eat the cake due to its peculiar taste.

From now on, suspicion not falls primarily on the two young women, who are increasingly under pressure. Finally, Sabine S. breaks down and makes a confession in the course of an intense interrogation. According to her, her sister Kathrin had ordered her to deposit the key to her parents' house in a certain newspaper box, which she did. This should have been their safeguard in case their parents would not open the door voluntarily.

From the moment the investigators confronted Kathrin S. with her sister's confession, she falls into profound silence.

Then Robert D., her fiancé, breaks down under the pressure and confesses that they met a young couple in a neighbouring town, Felix L. and Helga A., whom they commissioned to kill them. After the successful commitment of the crime, the five persons involved in the crime intended to divide the inheritance of the two adoptive daughters among themselves.

On the basis of this statement, an arrest warrant is immediately issued against the five conspirators.

At the end of the trial before the regional court, the judge sentences Felix L. and Robert D. to life imprisonment for murder out of greed. Since in the case of Felix L., a particular severity of the guilt was proven, an early release on probation for him is impossible and he will have no chance to get out of prison after 15 years.

Although the interrogations additionally led to the finding that Robert D. had already procured the rat poison for the first attempted murder of Karl and Maria S., he is convicted without any particular severity of guilt.

The verdict for Kathrin S. is: "Ten years in juvenile detention", which is the maximum sentence for juveniles. Sabine S. is imprisoned for seven years and ten months and Helga A. for seven years, taking into account her confession.

Justifying his decisions, the presiding judge states that the five accomplices committed the crime only because of the million-dollar inheritance and had nothing but dollar signs in their eyes during the preparation and execution of the deed.

Among other things, the interrogations had brought to light the plan of the five involved in the double murder: They intended to buy a restaurant in Mallorca from the heritage together and wanted to enjoy a carefree, worriless life in financial independence in the future.

Additionally, the presiding judge expresses his regret that Kathrin S. did not break her silence up until the end of the trial, and that she was the only one of the five accomplices who did not confess.

Her defence counsel, on the other hand, describes the verdict as disappointing and reserves the right to appeal after the trial. In fact, however, he does not realize the plan he announced, after he receives the written reasons for the decision.

On the day of their sentence, Kathrin and Sabine S. are both declared unworthy of inheritance. As a result, the relatives of the two murder victims inherit the assets and the business of Karl and Maria S.

For several years, the grand-nephew of the company founder gives his best to run the company and keep it alive after the family tragedy. This attempt fails in 2004 when the family business is forced to file for bankruptcy. At the auction sale of the remains of the traditional company, the last of the legendary kitchen appliances go under the hammer.

CHAPTER 7:
A Fateful Coincidence

Since the 26-year-old Sebastian K. takes part in a training course of the German Weather Service at a military airfield in southern Germany, he seldom comes home. The distance between the air base and his home town is more than 300 kilometres. For this reason, he thinks twice about whether the long weekend trip home is really worth it.

Since he completes this course for his long-awaited career advancement and for improving his family's financial situation, he assumes that his wife Christel shows understanding. He would be all too happy to spare her the trouble of having to wait tables in a bar in the evening.

On an ice-cold, cloudy day in February 1967, he receives a package at his training location from a sender completely unknown to him. At first, Sebastian K. is slightly bewildered. Is there some kind of mix-up? Did the post deliver the shipment to the wrong person?

Apparently not: on the brown wrapping paper wrapped around the box, his name is clearly readable. The complete address is correct, too.

At the end of his considerations, curiosity wins and Sebastian K. decides to open the mysterious package.

The unknown sender apparently does not seem to know him very well. Otherwise he wouldn't have enclosed a bottle of gentian schnapps with some chocolate probably everyone likes to eat. Sebastian K. never liked this spirit drink.

After placing the unloved bottle on the table, he discovers a handwritten note in the box. On this, the sender sends him greetings from the Palatinate, accompanied by an invitation to enjoy the beverage alone without any ruffle.

In the end, everything for Sebastian K. seems to indicate that an acquaintance is joking with him. Without pondering this any longer, he stores the strange package in his closet. Soon after, he already has forgotten about it.

The following Saturday, he visits his wife Christel and their two children. The hours spent together are as harmonious as ever and he stays with his resolution of not even mentioning the strange package. Still, he regrets having told some of his colleagues about it. Their sardonic remarks were enough for him. Who knows what ideas this story would give his wife?

After the almost traditional morning get-together

with his friend Klaus D. on Sunday morning, Sebastian K. returns to his training place. His 23-year-old roommate Rudi B. is lying there in bed with a severe cold.

When his unfortunate friend is still not feeling better the following Tuesday evening, Sebastian K. remembers the undesired bottle in his closet. Its label had a humorous saying on it that he just remembers. The message is that the contents of this bottle would provide health and vitality and replace the doctor.

In a spontaneous decision, he fills two glasses with the brew he finds so disgusting. If it helps his friend, the mysterious gift would at least serve a good purpose four days after its arrival.

The things you do for your friends! In order to keep the sick guy company, Sebastian K. as well puts the disgusting drink to his lips. But before he can swallow any of it, Rudi B. has already emptied his glass in one go.

"Yuck, that tastes like vinegar," his roommate says in disgust. Thereupon Sebastian K. finally abandons his courage and he gives up his plan to take a sip from his glass out of courtesy. Visibly relieved, he sets the glass down again.

Together the two friends go into the washroom to rinse out their mouths.

On the way back, everything happens quickly. Rudi B. can barely tell him that he feels a strong nausea. A few seconds later he collapses helplessly.

The emergency ambulance, which Sebastian K. immediately calls, arrives unexpectedly quickly. But for Rudi B. all help comes too late, he dies the same evening in a nearby hospital.

Later, forensic medicine finds that the cause of death was prussic acid poisoning.

The examination of the bottle confirms the logical conclusion that the toxic substance was present in the drink. Equally clear is the assumption that the poison was actually intended for Sebastian K. and that therefore, from the point of view of the murderer, the wrong person died.

As a result, the investigation is stalling for the time being. In the southern German city from which the parcel was mailed, the investors are able to track down the postal clerk who accepted the package. But he can't for the life of him remember the appearance of the woman who brought it to the post office. For reasons easily understandable, the investigation focuses on Sebastian K.'s family and his circle of acquaintances. During her interrogation, his wife Christel suspects that her still jealous ex-husband may be behind the assassination attempt.

At the same time, rumours reach the police that Christel K. for quite some time has had an affair with the 27-year-old car mechanic Andreas N. from her neighbourhood. According to these rumours, he seemingly did much more than just repairing her beloved, constantly broken car without end.

The decisive clue is finally provided by a witness who reports to the police because, a few weeks ago, he provided Andreas N. with the poison. Had he anticipated, at that time, what the poison, which he had easy access to at his workplace, actually was intended for, he would never have obliged his acquaintance. At least that's what he claims. Andreas N. supposedly told him that he wanted to get rid of a pesky marten.

Under the increasing pressure Christel K. and her lover Andreas N. finally admit that they sent the parcel. During their separate interrogations, the two suspects tell very different stories. They agree only on one point. They affirm again and again that they never intended to kill anyone. According to their allegations, Sebastian K. was only to be incapacitated for a while.

Nevertheless, with the arrest of the two suspects, the case seems to be solved. Contrary to the suspects' statements, the investigators conclude that the package was sent with the intention to get Sebastian K. out of the way.

Christel K. and Andreas N. continue to firmly deny this intention. They never make a comprehensive confession. Instead, they both try to present themselves as the victims who didn't know all the details of the other's plan and did not take him seriously enough.

The trial that is opened nine months later before the regional court is supposed to provide final clarity.

The fact that in the end, a completely uninvolved person fell victim to this assassination almost shocks the public even more than the deed itself.

In the course of the proceedings, Christel K. makes every effort to arouse pity with the description of her family background. All the time her father would have had other women and her mother would have had other men. At the beginning of her life, she supposedly had been ill for ten years. During this time, she was never allowed to leave the house to play with other children.

Consequently, her first marriage at the age of 17 supposedly was more something like an escape from her parental home. After her divorce she married Sebastian K., just like that without first getting to know him properly.

Christel K. has one child from her first marriage and another from her marriage with Sebastian K. In the courtroom, however, she does not at all create the impression of being a loving mother. Instead, she seems shockingly cold and calculating to everyone involved and her words and gestures seem more rehearsed than real.

Andreas N., an insignificant-looking small man, who not only had this one affair in the city, makes clear that he never intended to marry Christel K. After all, it is already enough for him to have to pay for his divorced wife. He wouldn't be stupid enough to saddle himself with Christel K.'s children, too.

According to his statement, the poison was merely intended to prevent Sebastian K. from coming home at the weekend thanks to a little diarrhoea.

And what's the man saying for whom the deadly drink was originally intended?

He is bewildered and steadfastly refuses to accept that his wife would have wanted to kill him. Maybe it's just too painful for him to allow that thought.

Why the defendants actually wanted to get Sebastian K. out of the way is another point the trial is unable to clarify. After all, he was rarely at home and didn't get in the way of their relationship at all. This incomprehensibly senseless act is and remains a mystery to everyone.

Finally, the court sentences Christel K. and Andreas N. to 15 years each for the attempted murder of Sebastian K. and for the negligent killing of Rudi B.

After having served two thirds of their sentence, they are released prematurely for good conduct. From then on, they go their separate ways. Neither of them will commit any crime after that.

CHAPTER 8:
Five Months Between Hope and Fear

Eight-year-old Maja W. is a curios and bright girl. Her father, a busy and wealthy attorney at a bank in a big city in the west of the country, and her mother, a versatile and talented artist, have fostered her daughter's interests and talents from the start on.

In this world, nothing means more to them than their child. Therefore, despite their above-average professional commitment, they do everything they can to ensure that it grows up in a loving environment where it can develop freely.

The fact that Maja W. is a happy girl radiates in all directions. When she smiles, the sun rises. She has many close friends and her classmates especially appreciate her gentleness and friendliness.

Of course, a child like Maja W. wants to prove as early as possible that it doesn't want be taken by the hand all the time. She is particularly proud of the fact that she finally can to go to school alone for a few weeks by now. It seems nothing can happen to her on the short footpath to her school in this quiet suburb surrounded by green.

On a frosty cold morning in December 1981, Maja W. cheerfully says goodbye to her parents. As she was dawdling around a bit that day, her girlfriends had already left before her. Maja doesn't care too much about that and she doesn't mind that there are hardly any other passers-by on that icy cold early morning.

Christmas is just around the corner and she is already looking forward to the great party and the holidays. On her way along the little-used road she imagines all the great things on her wish list. How many of her greatest wishes will come true in six days?

Suddenly the loud noise of squeaking brakes tears her out of her dreams. A large, dark car abruptly stops right next to her. Before Maja W. can form even a single clear thought, the back door of the car is torn open and two strong arms drag the girl inside the car. At the very same moment, the driver is speeding away at full throttle.

Her girlfriends at school are missing her. Is Maja sick today?

Even before classes start, one of Maja's best friends calls her mother, who immediately calls the police. Shortly afterwards, hundreds of policemen search the entire district, the riverbank and the surrounding parks. However, their efforts prove unsuccessful, Maja W. seems to have been disappeared off the face of the earth.

Her panicking parents don't have to wait long for the first clue. At noon on the same day, they receive a call from a suppressed number. When Maja's father answers the phone, he hears a tape recording playing. It tells them that their daughter has been kidnapped and that they under no circumstances must call the police. It is, however, already too late to meet this requirement at this point.

The next day, the postman delivers a letter from the kidnappers to Maja's parents. It contains the first instructions for handing over the ransom. The girl's father is supposed to contact the kidnappers on a certain radio frequency at the river bank at specific times. They will then answer him by mail.

As proof that Maja is actually in the hands of the blackmailers, they enclosed a hair clip of the girl with their letter.

From the outset, this case differs from the usual procedure for other kidnappings, in that the blackmailers do not mention a specific amount of ransom. Instead, they ask how much their daughter's life is worth to the frightened parents.

Three days later, Maja's father offers the kidnappers 800,000 DM. They accept this amount without any hesitation. However, they point out that with each failed ransom handover attempt, this sum will increase by 50,000 DM.

On Christmas Eve, the first attempt on a train fails. Most likely, the blackmailers observe that Maja's father gets on the train accompanied by several plain-clothed policemen. That's why the kidnappers won't report again that day.

For Maja's parents, this is the beginning of an almost unbearable up and down, a horrible nightmare between hope and fear.

In the course of the following weeks and months, numerous further attempts to pay the ransom fail, including two failed drops of the money by helicopter. The first time, the agreed radio signal is not received and the second time the helicopter takes off too late because the police are still waiting for a reconnaissance plane.

As the kidnappers had announced previously, the amount of their claim is increasing with each failure.

Over the same period, at intervals, parents receive new life-signs from their daughter, such as a tape-recorder tape, which underlines the kidnappers' demands, and a letter written by Maja.

On New Year's Day 1982, Maja's parents address the public in a radio broadcast. They offer a reward of 100,000 DM for relevant information about the whereabouts of their daughter.

In February 1982 the family is at the end of its rope. It authorizes a large-scale police investigation and raises the amount of the advertised reward to 250,000 DM. They receive hundreds of clues from the population, but no one puts the investigators on a useful track.

Four weeks later, the desperate parents see no other way but to withdraw the promised reward and call on the police to stop the investigation. From now on, it doesn't matter to them whether the kidnappers of her daughter will be brought to justice for their crime one day. All they care about now is Maja's release.

During the time seemingly never-ending time since the kidnapping of the eight-year-old girl, Maja's parents more and more have lost confidence in the police. From this point on, they no longer inform investigators about the further course of events. Instead, they bring in private mediators, a journalist with extensive experience in this field and a former director of the Federal Criminal Police Office.

In March 1982, 500 people in Maja's hometown pray together that the girl will return home safe and sound.

Meanwhile, the mediators communicate with the kidnappers via newspaper advertisements, the ransom demand has increased to 1.5 million DM. This means that it now has almost doubled from the amount originally agreed upon.

In May 1982, one of the two mediators throws the ransom from a moving train in response to an agreed signal. This time the hand-over is successful. After that, Maja's parents suffer for three further endless days until one of the employees of a motorway service area discovers Maja W. by chance in front of the building. That's where the kidnappers had taken her in the trunk of a car.

A sigh of relief goes through all of Germany. For 149 horrible days, Maja's parents continually have gone through hell. Now they finally can take their beloved daughter back into their arms. The girl is weak but healthy and unharmed as if by a miracle.

The overjoyed parents only slowly and gradually understand that they are not only dreaming.

What follows this nightmare almost sounds too good to be true. Soon, Maja W. goes back to school, where she does her best to catch up on the material she missed.

For a certain time she is still cared for by doctors and psychologists, but this is not necessary for too long.

Step by step, the eight-year-old girl finds the strength to talk about her experiences. Maja W. tells her parents that during her imprisonment she was guarded by two people, a woman and a man, in a darkened room illuminated only by a flashlight. According to her, she was never abused or threatened and not even tied up. Her kidnappers even tried to establish a friendly relationship with her. For example, she was allowed to write and paint and was regularly supplied with books, fairy tapes and comic books.

The public is informed about Maja's detailed descriptions of the hiding place of the kidnappers in a well-known television programme. However, the incoming calls do not offer any leads.

What happened to the ransom also remains a mystery to this day. Some of the banknotes with registered numbers are found by children in a forest in December 1982. At about the same time, four men try to exchange 400,000 DM of the ransom in Turkey. When they are arrested, they also claim to have discovered the money in a forest. Since they don't even come close to the intelligence, local knowledge and cold-bloodedness of the kidnappers, it quickly turns out they actually have nothing to do with the crime.

Most likely the remaining ransom is put about abroad.

Despite the intensive investigation, there is still no decisive evidence to this day of the identity of Maja W.'s kidnappers. They are still at large.

Today, Maja W. lives with her family in another town. Years ago, her father told the public that the case was closed for his entire family and that they would never want to be contacted again about it.

CHAPTER 9:
A Cruelty Well Insured

Like countless other girls, Susanne T., who grew up in the countryside, is already completely besotted with horses at a very young age. In contrast to most people who share this love with her, however, she is very lucky to get an apprenticeship as a horse farmer on a farm in the north-east of the country.

From the first day on she takes the farm's animals into her heart. With absolute certainty she knows she has found her dream job.

At work in spring 2011, the pretty young woman meets Mario P., who is two years older than her. Since he participates as a rider in jumping tournaments, they quickly find a common thread. With Mario P., Susanne T. can talk endlessly about horses. One day she is surprised to realize she has fallen hopelessly in love with the likeable, handsome man.

When she feels that he is feeling the same, 21-year-old Susanne T. is on cloud nine. Life couldn't possibly be any better.

Soon, the young couple begins to dream of a common future on their own horse farm. The two of them expect happiness and wealth from breeding and selling noble horses.

In order to start realising their plans, they move to a horse farm in the same federal state in autumn 2011. Susanne T. would never have believed before that everything would work out so smoothly. But this is only possible because Anita P. has leased the farm to support her son. As a well-earning financial advisor at a bank, Mario's mother thinks is able to afford this luxury.

Because she underestimated the total monthly costs, she however finds herself in financial struggle after only a few weeks. In her awkward situation, she cannot pay the rent nor can she pay the current bills for ancillary costs, car insurance and the veterinarian. As expected, the farm owner immediately terminates the contract.

The unconditional love of Susanne T. for Mario P. is, however, not affected by these setbacks. Following their engagement in November 2011, she is persuaded by her lover to take out a term life insurance policy for about 250,000 Euro. Knowing that her future husband will at least be financially secure in the event of her death reassures her profoundly.

After the medical examination required for the insurance provides no obstacles, Susanne T. signs the contract at the beginning of December 2011.

But apparently this still isn't enough for Anita and Mario P. In the same month, mother and son conclude seven additional term life insurance policies with various insurance companies through a broker in the name of Susanne T. In each of these contracts Mario P. is registered as the beneficiary. In the event of the death of Susanne T., this results in a total sum of more than two million Euro that would be paid to her fiancé.

Even so, Susanne T. does not suspect the slightest of these additional contracts. They were all sealed with her forged signature without her knowledge.

These contracts are the starting signal for a series of attempted murders.

One evening in April 2012, Mario P. drives to a petrol station that is monitored with a video camera in order to obtain a watertight alibi. Meanwhile, at home, his mother out of the blue stabs Susanne T. in the back. As if by some miracle, none of her internal organs are injured by this attack. Completely shocked, confused and disoriented, Susanne T. defends herself until Anita P. flees.

When Mario P. returns, he takes his fiancée to a hospital where she is treated in intensive care for several days.

After her recovery, Susanne T. moves back to her parents and files charges against Anita P.

During her interrogation, Mario P.'s mother testifies she had suffered a kind of blackout that evening. Since the investigators now assume that Anita P. was in a mentally disturbed state at the time of the act, the proceedings for grievous bodily harm are discontinued after a short time.

Despite this traumatic experience, Susanne T. does not break off contact with her fiancé. She takes him to be completely innocent and unsuspecting.

In June 2012, Mario P. meets the 20-year-old hobby rider Melissa M., who falls in love with him head over heels. He quickly learns how to manipulate her feelings by promising her a common future and urging her to poison his fiancée Susanne T. In return, he promises her an additional reward of 50,000 Euro.

The inexperienced young woman is stupid and ruthless enough to get involved and meets Susanne T. in a parking lot. She leads her to believe she wants to buy a horse from her. The champagne she offers Susanne T. in a plastic cup contains potassium chloride, which Mario P. bought from a pharmacy.

As potassium chloride has to be injected into the bloodstream for a deadly reaction, this second murder attempt also fails.

Later, Anita P. testifies that her son did not know about the attack and purchased potassium chloride as a dietary supplement for his horses.

Following the unwelcome failure, Melissa M. asks her brother Sebastian, who lives in a large West German city, to get her in contact with an acquaintance that would be willing to commit a contract murder. Without hesitation, Sebastian M., convicted several times, introduces her to the 22-year-old Klaus C., who has also been convicted of minor offences. He demands a payment of 500 Euro and accepts the job without hesitation.

On a warm summer night in June 2012, Mario P. stays overnight with Susanne T. in her parents' house. From there, he sends an SMS to Melissa M. with roughly the following content: "We cannot afford a third failure."

For the evening of the following day Mario P. arranges a meeting with Susanne T. on the parking lot of an outdoor swimming pool. There, Klaus C. waits in his hiding place for his target to appear.

When Susanne T. arrives at the agreed meeting point around 10 PM, Klaus C. attacks her immediately. While he strangles her with a rope, Mario P. and Melissa and Sebastian M. watch the victim's several minutes-long agony from close range.

The next morning, a walker discovers the body of Susanne T. in the parking lot.

When the investigations begin, the police assume that this is most probably a relationship crime. For this reason, the investigators concentrate on Mario P., whom they take into custody as a suspect.

A week later, Klaus C. is also arrested after he bragged about his crime in front of several witnesses in his home town.

In the further course of the investigations, Mario and Anita P.'s financial problems increasingly come to the fore. As a result, Anita P. is also arrested two weeks later.

Each new finding more and more leads the investigators to believe that Susanne T. was murdered insidiously and brutally out of pure greed.

In March 2013 the trial against the alleged perpetrators opens before the regional court. The victim's parents appear as joint plaintiffs.

With their statements in court, those involved in the murder plot incriminate each other until Melissa M. can no longer withstand the pressure and gives a comprehensive confession.

As the reason for her decision she states that she wanted to get the terrible pictures out of her head. She describes herself as an unstable woman who would have done anything to win Mario P.'s affection, without exception.

Only her detailed description of the entire course of events provides final clarity.

On this basis, at the end of January 2015, the regional court sentences Mario and Anita P. to life imprisonment for murder and two attempted murders with a particular severity of guilt. Since the court regards them as the two masterminds behind the horrible crimes, there is no hope of parole for them after 15 years.

The court declares Klaus C. and Sebastian M. guilty of murder and incitement to murder. For them, too, a life sentence waits.

As Melissa M.'s confession played a decisive role in clarifying the course of events completely, the court sentences her to fourteen years and six months imprisonment for murder and attempted murder. In support of that order, the court holds that she had been manipulated and used by Mario P.

The verdicts become final in 2016.
Out of pure greed for money and with a cold-heart-edness that is hard to beat, a young life was wiped out without flinching. What greed can drive some people to is often far more shocking than any fictional story could ever be.

CHAPTER 10:
Choked Childhood Dreams

That girl, terrifyingly small and fragile for her age, hasn't yet seen much more than her own room in her parents' flat in an eight-story residential block. She would have to go outside to find friends and play with them. But she's not supposed to.

So, the seven-year-old Maja F. from a North German city dreams day by day, escapes from the confines of her own four walls into another world. In her imagination she can laugh and dance, jump and run, and do all the wonderful things that make other children happy at her age.

When you dream, you don't cause unwelcome noises and you don't disturb anyone.

Under no circumstances, she wants to annoy her parents, 35-year-old Helga F. and 49-year-old Tobias W.

Neither do her parents count themselves among the lucky ones born into a privileged social environment. Helga F. never met her father. Her mother was an alcoholic. That's why she did not intervene when her former partner regularly harassed her daughter from the age of nine on.

Shortly after her 13th birthday, Helga F. escaped from her parents' house to live with her aunt. She dropped out of her hairstylist training prematurely because of an allergy.

After marrying in 1991 at the age of 21, Helga F. gave birth to two sons and a daughter over the course of four years. Since she was extremely neglectful of her children, her aunt brought in the youth welfare office. As a result, Helga F.'s eldest son was given up for adoption and, after her divorce in 1996, the father was granted custody of the two younger children.

Helga F. lost her job as a seamstress very soon afterwards because she was constantly absent without excuse.

A few months after her divorce, she met Tobias W., a painter and varnisher who had just moved in from another big city. About a year later, her daughter Maja was born, unwanted by both parents.

So much for the little girl's sad family background. Let's now return to the year 2005, in which Maja F. is seven years old!

On a cold, rainy morning in March 2005, Helga F. calls the emergency doctor. She claims her daughter vomited during the night and has been unconscious ever since.

When the ambulance arrives, there's nothing more

the emergency doctor can do for Maja. She's been dead so long rigor mortis has already set in. The small, wasted body weighs only 9.6 kilograms at this point.

Not only this deeply shocks the emergency doctor as it shocks as the investigators arriving shortly afterwards. Added to this, the whole apartment is in an almost unimaginably neglected condition.

Maja's father claims that his daughter had a metabolic disorder. However, she was not under medical treatment.

During the autopsy of the girl, the forensic pathologist finds that Maja F. had suffered a life-threatening intestinal obstruction due to permanent malnutrition. On the evening before the emergency call was received, the child had vomited while eating. As it was already much too weak at this point to free its airways by itself, it suffocated on its vomit. There were no life-threatening pre-existing conditions. But the child was in such a bad physical condition that it couldn't have been awake for quite some time. There's a good chance it was just in a semiconscious state.

What the subsequent investigations reveal is almost inconceivable.

Several neighbours testify that they had never seen the little girl before and did not even know that she existed at all.

Her parents had her permanently locked in her room. Only in a few exceptional cases they permitted her daughter to go to the toilet, and she was given something to eat and drink only extremely rarely and irregularly.

The investigators don't find a single toy in her former room. The windows of the room are screwed shut and the glass panes are covered with a foil preventing daylight from entering the room. The ceiling is covered with mould, and from the mattress the little girl slept on only the springs are left. The heater is set to the lowest setting and the lamp doesn't work.

Tobias W. had already removed the carpet and the linoleum on the floor some time ago. Using a copper wire without the necessary insulation, he transformed the light switch into a life-threatening safety hazard.

Yet he decidedly denies that he ever had any intention of killing his daughter. According to him, the girl would have torn off the protective cover of the light switch herself.

An expert opinion, however, confirms the investigators' suspicions.

In the course of the investigations, the persons in charge of the case fight with tears not only once. It almost felt like a fortunate coincidence of fate that Maja F. was finally delivered from her suffering that had lasted for so many years.

The girl is buried in silence ten days after her death. Her parents were already arrested on the day the body was discovered. Due to the danger of flight, the judge orders them to remain in investigative custody.

During the interrogations, Helga F. testifies that she had fed and cared for her daughter regularly. She excuses her wrongdoings with her own difficult childhood.

Tobias W. admits not having taken care of his child anymore since the end of last year, as it would have obviously rejected him. At the beginning of 2005, he saw Maja alive for the last time.

In June 2005, the public prosecutor's office presses charges against the girl's parents. They are accused of mistreating a ward and of murder by omission. Through their guilt, Maja F. was denied the chance to develop physically and mentally in the way appropriate to her age.

In addition, there is the suspicion that Helga F. and Tobias W. have agreed to let their child die in order to cover up their earlier crimes.

In the course of the investigation, neither the father nor the mother show even a hint of remorse or insight.

The trial against the parents is opened before the regional court in August 2005. Not until the second day of the trial, Helga F. admits she neglected her daughter and locked her in her room. Since February 2005, Maja increasingly refused food and drink. As Tobias W. had suffered from liver cirrhosis since 2003, the relationship between him and his daughter supposedly worsened even further. For this reason Maja F. would have completely withdrawn into herself. However, she herself would not have been able to visit a doctor or a child guidance centre.

Tobias W. does not break his persistent silence even in court.

The psychological expert comes to the conclusion that the defendants are shockingly cold, but do not suffer from any mental illness. The conclusion is therefore that both are criminally liable.

Although the parents' defender demands a lighter sentence for bodily harm resulting in death as well as ill-treatment, in November 2005, the district court sentences Helga F. and Tobias W. to life imprisonment for murder by omission with the characteristic of cruelty.

In support of his decision, the judge states that the defendants had even treated their cat better than their own child, to whom they refused any form of care. He was convinced they approvingly accepted the death of their daughter.

What this process brought to light is shocking the public. At the same time, the responsible authorities find themselves caught in the crossfire of criticism.

Why did the youth welfare office ignore the prehistory of the three older children of Helga F. and did not take care of the girl?

Maja F. has been required to attend school since August 2004.The parents did not respond to the three letters of the headteacher requesting the parents to register their child at school. Therefore, the headteacher reported the absence of the girl to the school board. Employees of the school board overall made three futile attempts to find the family in their homes. They also received no reply to their letters. As a result, the board demanded a fine of 60 Euro from the parents. Since this was never paid and the subsequent reminders did not produce any reaction, the school board assumed that the family had moved. On the basis of this assumption, they stopped their efforts and the responsible youth welfare office was never informed about the case.

These inconceivable findings trigger a fierce public debate. The responsible authorities justify their complete failure mainly with the constant lack of personnel, the lack of appropriately trained specialists and the excessive costs which would result from appropriate measures to protect children.

Ultimately, the sad fate of Maja F. leads to the extension of state control mechanisms and to an increase in personnel and funds for the relevant authorities. In 2008, a new law on the protection of the child's well-being is passed at the federal level.

For Maja, however, these urgently needed measures unfortunately come too late.

CHAPTER 11:
Honour Killing

18-year-old Djamila A. is a child of our time. Her parents, Fatma and Kerim A., come from rural Anatolia and immigrated to Germany in the beginning 1990s. With this step, which was not easy for them, they hoped to provide a better future for themselves and especially for their children.

In the West German city they have been living in for more than twenty years now, they have settled in well after some initial difficulties.

Here, Djamila A. is born in 1993 as one of the family's ten children. The fact that she grows up bilingual promises her considerable advantages for her coming life.

Everyone in the neighbourhood is enchanted by the smile of that cute little girl with the black pigtails and the big dark eyes. At school Djamila A., who is as kind as she is curios, gets to know many German children right from the start. Some of these children become close friends for her.

Her parents raise her much more strictly than her peers, but that doesn't bother her all that much. As soon as she leaves home, she acts like everyone else. Basically, she lives between two worlds all the time. So why shouldn't she succeed in making the most of the combination of these two worlds for herself?

In her hometown she successfully attends comprehensive school until 2010. In order to earn her own money and to be able to fulfil at least some of her greatest wishes, she then works in a bakery. At the age of 18, she meets the 23-year-old Russian-German Igor J. there. It's love at first sight for the two young people.

When her family finds out about her relationship, they react with anything but understanding. Because of their religion, Djamila's parents are unable to accept that she loves a man from another culture. For them, her daughter is a disgrace to the entire family.

For this reason Djamila A. is threatened and insulted by her family. Her father strictly forbids her to see this man again even once. But the self-confident young woman cannot and will not bow to this. It hurts her to have to disappoint her parents, but the voice of her heart nevertheless prevails.

As soon as her father has to realize that he won't achieve anything with his prohibitions and threats, a time of suffering begins for Djamila A. What the family couldn't achieve with words, they now intend to achieve by force.

Again and again, Djamila A. is locked up at home and beaten by her father Kerim A. and her older brother Amir A.

After all, Djamila A. sees no other way out than to flee to a women's shelter and break away from her family. In order not to be found, she even changes her name, hair style and colour.

Her love for Igor J. gives her the strength she desperately needs in these testing times.

At the beginning of November 2011, Djamia A. spends a carefree and happy day with her lover after which she does not return to the women's shelter. Shortly after midnight, the young couple is suddenly woken by deafening noise. Frightened to death, the two notice that four brothers and a sister of Djamila A. have forcefully entered Igor J.'s apartment. They brutally force their sister to come with them.

Igor J. is helpless against the superiority of the intruders, but he informs the police immediately after the attack.

On the same day, the investigators succeed in arresting all the siblings of Djamila A. involved in the crime at two different locations and put them in custody on remand.

Djamila A. remains missing without a trace after the attack.

In the course of the interrogations, the siblings remain silent. Supposedly none of them knows anything about the current whereabouts of Djamila A.

The night following the break-in in Igor J.'s apartment, several witnesses from a nearby forest heard shots. These statements trigger a large-scale search operation that also includes a police helicopter. Since this does not lead to any result, however, investigators initially suspect that Djamila A. was kidnapped and brought abroad.

Therefore, they ask foreign authorities for their assistance. When these measures remain unsuccessful, investigators no longer rule out that the girl might have been killed.

In mid-December, the police asked the public for relevant information on a well-known television programme. The public prosecutor's office promises a reward of 5,000 Euro for these.

Not until January 2012, an employee of a golf club discovers the body of Djamila A. on a golf course. He alerts the police immediately.

This gruesome find causes Djamila A.'s brother Malik to break his silence and describe the course of events as far as he knows. For being the only one testifying, he is released from custody on parole.

Three weeks later Djamila A. is buried in her parents' home village. About thirty mourners attend the funeral. Her parents stay away from the ceremony.

At the beginning of March 2012, the public prosecutor's office presses charges against the five siblings involved in taking the victim hostage. Three of them have to answer for murder or accessory to murder.

The psychological expert appointed by the court

explains that the family's faith wouldn't tolerate a love affair with a person of a different religion. Moreover, it is the family's conviction that women have to be virgins when they marry. The failure of a single family member would be regarded as the failure of the entire family. But apparently there wasn't a single indication of a sudden irrational act and all five siblings were culpable.

Already on the first day of the trial, 22-year-old Amir A. confesses. Because his sister had insulted and spat at him, he wouldn't have been in control of himself anymore and would have killed Djamila A. with two head shots.

Still, doubts remain. The presiding judge suspects that Amir A. possibly confesses the crime only to protect other family members.

Sister Melina A., involved in the kidnapping, claims that the murder wasn't planned beforehand. Originally, they had intended to take Djamila A. to one of their uncles using the family car. When she had stayed in the car for a short break on the way, she suddenly heard two shots.

However, she herself would have been the driving force behind the kidnapping. As an employee of the city, she would have had access to the residents' registration office data. This allowed her to find out the address where her sister Djamila was staying.

Owing to this statement, Melina A. is immediately dismissed by her employer.

Several former fellow prisoners of Malik A. withdraw their statements at the last minute after they were threatened in prison.

At the same time, there are rumours that Malik A. wants nothing more to do with his family. Therefore, he would have asked the investigators to include him in a witness protection program.

The parents of the accused, Malik A.'s wife and a cousin refuse to testify.

As additional evidence emerges, Kerim A., the father of Djamila, is now also being investigated.

In May 2012, the Regional Court sentences Amir A. to life imprisonment for murder. For Melina A. and another brother involved in the crime, a ten-year prison sentence waits for taking hostages, aiding and accessory murder. In the case of Malik A. and the other brother involved in the kidnapping, the court agrees on a five-and-a-half-year prison sentence for taking hostages.

In his explanatory statement to these verdicts, the presiding judge clarified that Djamila A. was executed with two targeted shots to the head. All this wouldn't have been about disputes within the family, but about a planned "honour murder".

Until today, the place where Djamila A. died hasn't been determined. The murder weapon was never found.

In November 2012, the court presses charges against Kerim A., the father of the murdered girl. In January 2013, the trial against him for inciting murder and grievous bodily harm begins. At the beginning of February 2013, the 53-year-old defendant is sentenced to six and a half years in prison for accessory to murder by omission and grievous bodily harm.

Fatma A., the mother of the murder victim, must answer to the regional court in July 2013 for dangerous assault, deprivation of liberty and coercion of her daughter. She gets off with a year's imprisonment on probation and 80 hours of community service.

How the individual family members are able continue to live with the heavy burden of their guilt is beyond the imagination of all loving parents and siblings.

CHAPTER 12:
An Insidious Trap

About two and a half hours after midnight in October 1991, the police of an idyllic small town in the west of the country receive an emergency call. It originates from an emergency telephone on a parking lot in the woods near a highway. Therefore it is mainly used by hikers during the day.

When the officer of the night's watch answers the call, he hears a male voice stammering slightly. The nightly caller gives the following information: "Good day! My name is Meyer. I just had a wildlife accident. Nobody was injured, but my bumper was slightly damaged. Would you please send someone over?"

In the course of his numerous years of service, the police officer already has experienced a lot in his night shifts. In his opinion, this emergency call requires nothing more than the usual routine. Completely unconcerned, he informs his colleagues from the small town closest to the car park who are responsible for wildlife accidents in this area.

Police sergeant Peter V. and Axel P. are also on duty that night. A quarter of an hour ago they took a driver to the hospital that had to undergo a blood test after a routine traffic check. Since the two colleagues are both fathers of families, they are already looking forward to the approaching morning. After their shifts, each of them will sit at the breakfast table with his wife and two children to finish off the tiring night duty in a pleasant way.

From the hospital which they are now standing in front of, it's not far to the parking lot in the forest. After receiving the emergency call from the operations centre, they take off immediately with their civilian patrol car. Silently, they both hope they will accomplish their final task before the end of their service early in the morning.

After they have taken off, contact with them breaks off.

One and a half hours later, the chief of operation still hasn't received any response from them. He's finally starting to get restless. After all, he has known Peter V. and Axel P. for years as a perfectly coordinated team on which he can rely completely. Suspecting they might have had an accident or a breakdown on the way, he sends a second patrol car off to look for the colleagues.

The two patrolmen arrive at the parking lot in the forest right before dawn. In the darkness, they at first discover no hint that Peter V. and Axel P. ever were here.

Slightly confused, they grab their flashlights out of the car. Suddenly, in the bushes at the edge of the parking lot, their lights reveal signs of a disaster. On the ground they see empty cartridge casings, traces of blood and tissue, and bone and tooth splinters. What might have happened here?

Around 10:00 AM at a nearby military training area, a hunter stumbles upon the vehicle of the missing officers, completely burnt-out. The sides of the car wreck have numerous bullet holes. Peter V. and Axel P. themselves, however, seem to have disappeared off the face of the earth.

Their mysterious disappearance immediately triggers one of the biggest search operations ever conducted in Germany. Almost 6,000 civil servants from three different federal states and divers participate, searching the river near the crime scene. But the large search operation doesn't lead to any results either.

In the face of this terrible uncertainty, it proves to be a true stroke of luck that all inbound emergency calls are recorded automatically.

With a request for relevant information, the police set up a telephone number where the public can listen to the call of the supposed "Mr Meyer". Hundreds of alleged witnesses report as a result.

Although a neighbour of the perpetrator recognizes the voice and a reward of 50,000 DM is on offer, the witness doesn't dare to contact the police for fear of his own safety.

Ultimately, the decisive information comes from several prison officers and prisoners of the correctional facility, from which the 29-year-old Volker K. had been released prematurely only a few weeks earlier for good behaviour. The witnesses unanimously identify the voice of the small-time criminal, who served the majority of his ten-month prison sentence in this institution.

Four days after the disappearance of Peter V. and Axel P., a police task force storms the house where Volker K. and his two brothers are staying. Thanks to the effect of surprise, the suspect and his brother, Robert K., are overwhelmed and do not offer any resistance. Panicking, the third brother, Herbert K., attempts suicide by stabbing his own chest and neck with a knife two times.

During the subsequent house search, the officers find an assault rifle with telescopic sight, two machine guns and the corresponding ammunition in the attic.

After his 25-year-old brother Robert has burdened him with his confession, Volker K. can no longer withstand the increasing pressure of the interrogations. About a week after the crime, he leads the investigators to the place in the forest where the bodies of Peter V. and Axel P. were buried in a densely overgrown conifer plantation.

Without any warning, the two officers were killed by a total of thirteen shots from a distance of less than seven metres as soon they arrived at the parking lot in the woods. The assault rifle from the attic of the house of the three brothers is clearly identified as the murder weapon.

Later, the investigators discover a second hiding place near the home of the K. brothers, which contains, among other things, the service weapons of the two murdered policemen and large quantities of ammunition.

During the trial, which lasted 180 days and was opened in 1992 before the regional court, Herbert K. severely incriminated his brother Volker. In his statements he presents him as the decisive force behind the crime. Although Robert K. more and more contradicts himself, his participation in the crime cannot be proven.

Regarding the weapons and ammunition found in the brothers' house and the hiding place, clear evidence is provided during the trial that the K. brothers committed other serious crimes beforehand.

Among other things, this involved a raid on a German army barrack in December 1986, a theft on a military training area in April 1987, a robbery on a German army patrol in April 1987 including a firefight, and a raid on another German army barrack in May 1988. After they had knocked down a guard with a club, this raid also resulted in a firefight.

In all these crimes, the brothers K. stole weapons, ammunition and equipment of the German army.

In total, the trial against the brothers K. costs more than one million DM.

In February 1995, the Regional Court sentenced

Volker K. to life imprisonment for murder with a particularly severity of guilt. In addition, the judge orders that Volker K. be taken into safe custody because of his exceptional dangerousness. The minimum time for serving his sentence is set to 25 years.

In the text of the decision, the court states that the perpetrator's motive was solely his general hatred of the police.

Herbert K. awaits a ten-year prison sentence for accessory to murder and accessory to serious robbery. Because of the lack of evidence, Robert K. is acquitted of the suspicion of accessory to murder. He is sentenced to a two-year suspended prison sentence for his involvement in the raids on the German army barracks and for aiding and abetting serious robbery.

After his retirement in 2016, one of the former investigators in charge of this devastating murder case makes a public statement. On the basis of Robert K.'s interrogations, he is convinced that Volker K.'s motive would have been much more than just his general hatred of police officers. Instead, Volker K.'s abysmal hatred would have been directed against a particular policeman who was investigating him for various crimes. This hostility would have led to his plan to take revenge on this specific official. A certain television series served him as a model for his deed. His actual goal would have been to stage the murder of the police officer as an alleged suicide and to capture his service weapon.

The other persons involved in the investigations at that time and in the trial are unable confirm this perspective.

Volker K. remains in custody to this day.

His brothers Robert and Herbert K. now live under different names in the vicinity of their former hometown.

In memory of the two murdered policemen, a memorial stone was erected on the parking lot in the forest.

With their choice of career, two young family fathers had decided to protect their fellows. In the end, they had to pay for their choice with their own lives.

CHAPTER 13:
In Love, Engaged, Married, Dead.

At the age of 44, Barbara F., born in 1939, already looks back on a life full of events.

During the war she fled from Upper Silesia to Germany with her family, where she marries in 1961. Three years later she regrets her hasty step with her first divorce.

For a while she works as a geriatric nurse. Her salary for this activity, however, not even remotely meets her unrealistically high material demands. So she has to look for a more lucrative alternative.

In 1971, she marries Daniel G., with whom she opened three bars in various rural villages over the following years. In reality, however, these bars are brothels. Maybe, she thinks, she can this way make the fast buck she has dreamed of all her life.

When this doesn't work out either, she offers her own body to the male visitors of her bar in a caravan next to the building.

Soon her second marriage has come to an end. Many

years later she tells that she had been constantly abused and beaten by Daniel G. After this experience she would have had enough of young men. From then on, she wants her peace.

Consequently, Barbara F. decides to concentrate exclusively on older men in the future. If these feel the urgent desire to finance her expensive travels and cars or to sign their own house over to her, that wouldn't be a problem after all. On the contrary! You don't turn down gifts just out of politeness.

That's her version of the story, at least. When her son Tobias G. is asked about it many years later, he draws a different picture. He remembers that his mother had stated that most older men were wealthy. With a little skilfulness, she'd inherit their fortune after their death. Compared to drudging in the retirement home that would be a nice thing. But when the old gentlemen were hot for her in the end, she found it disgusting.

In order to put her plan into action, Barbara F. places contact ads. In 1983, 82-year-old Otto S. is the first man to fall for her. He hardly believes his luck when the much younger, attractive and fun-loving woman shows interest for him.

Even before the end of 1985, he has declared her his sole heir in his will and transferred eleven plots of land to her. He dies in January 1986.

Although he died in hospital, his relatives start to ask unpleasant questions. Something wasn't right as the recently healthy dand agile Otto S. suddenly felt unwell. Investigations are initiated on the basis of these statements and of the unclear cause of death. As these do produce any results, the proceedings are discontinued in the same year.

The 77-year-old master bricklayer Karl M. is the second man falling into the trap of the black widow. After answering his contact ad, Barbara F. writes him ardent love letters. She also visits him regularly and presents herself to the neighbours in his village, scantily dressed, in his garden. When he completely lost his mind over her in love, he gives her large amounts of cash, a Mercedes and treats her with several luxury trips.

Following the death of Karl M., his children, living in another federal state, file a charge. They are certain that Barbara F. has treacherously deprived their father of his savings and poisoned him little by little. But this charge, too, leads to no nothing.

The 83-year-old Werner T., Barbara F.'s third husband, is killed by two men during in a robbery in his apartment in February 1991. At the time of his death, he was married to Barbara F. for just half a year. After this tragic incident, no suspicion falls on the grieving widow.

Husband number four, Albert N. from a West German city, 87 years old at the time of her first encounter, Barbara F. meets in Spain. That's because she now has expanded her hunting ground into the south. She fleeces Albert N. thoroughly as well. However, he has the rare luck of staying alive for nine years after his one-and-a-half year marriage to Barbara F. Exceptions prove the rule.

Barbara F. doesn't think about it. For her, the man-hunt just keeps going on, beat by beat.

From the money she earns with her new "job", Barbara F. buys a two-building estate in a small community in the north-west part of the country.

From now on she accommodates most of the men who fall for her ads there. Among other things, she describes herself in her advertisements as a widow, wanting to look after elderly men in need of care.

Those who decide to be lovingly looked after by Barbara F. soon die without a single cent in their pocket. Over the years, she takes a total of more than 670,000 Euro from seniors who fall into her trap looking for late luck.

Only one of the men Barbara F. meets during this time stays with her. This is the welfare recipient alcoholic Konrad C. to whom she had lent a smaller sum some time ago. Since then he has lived in a garden house close to her estate to serve as her servant and court hand.

In 1990 something completely unexpected happens that never had a place in Barbara F.'s plans. Head over heels she falls in love with 50-year-old Thorsten B., a former German army member. This time it goes the other way around; it's her who is suddenly the one financing her lover's holiday trips and a car.

Nevertheless, she's not giving up her forays through the whole of Germany. One day she says goodbye to Thorsten B. with the words: "I just have to quickly inherit a grandfather's inheritance."

Completely shocked, Thorsten B. immediately gives her the sack. Shortly thereafter, he reports her to the police, but also this investigation is stopped and the file is destroyed.

To forget her heartache, Barbara F. lures evermore victims into her web.

Not until August 2007 tides turn out of the blue. The police have ordered Konrad C. to the station. Barbara F. is constantly in conflict with her neighbours, whom she occasionally likes to report. Konrad C. now has to make a statement regarding one of these cases.

In the countryside, police officers know every single member of the village community. Therefore it surprises them immensely that Konrad C. appears soberly, cleanly and neatly dressed on the station this morning. They have no idea yet that Konrad C. would like to clear things on this day.

His introductory sentence: "When we're done here, you'll need your handcuffs," sets off an avalanche. He talks and talks – and does that for several weeks. It seems he finally wants to free himself from the dependence on Barbara F. and draw a final line. In the meantime, in a painful process, he has understood that this woman could never replace the family he never had. Besides, he's afraid she's going to poison him, too, eventually.

"The money and all that shit drove her crazy," explains Konrad C.

Without hesitation, he also reveals all the details of his aiding and abetting her crimes.

Only gradually the officials begin to understand that a new chapter in German criminal history is being written right in their office. Over a period of more than twenty years, the accused systematically fleeced older men and killed most of them.
Investigators hardly believe their ears.
Following the shocking statements of Konrad C., Barbara F.'s son Tobias G. is asked for questioning. After all, his mother is also fighting a bitter legal battle against him for custody of her granddaughter.
Tobias G. says that his mother's men were mostly in good physical condition when they arrived. Soon, however, they would start to become weaker from day to day until they were only able to lie in bed. Mainly this would probably have been due to the psychotropic drugs that his mother had a doctor prescribed her in order to mix them with the food of these men. Additionally, these drugs had the welcome side effect of making the men even more submissive and generous.
In the course of the extensive investigations, Barbara F. is without any doubt proven to have committed four murders between 1994 and 2000. In at least eight further deaths she is strongly suspected of having committed an offence. In the end, however, the evidences are not sufficient in these cases.
Without exception, she sedated her victims using medication. If this did not lead to their death fast enough, Barbara F. helped by strangling the defenceless seniors or suffocating them with a pillow or a

plastic bag. In several cases she was assisted by Konrad C., who was diminished guilty due to his mental condition. Some of the bodies were burned or buried.

In 2009, the regional court sentences the 69-year-old Barbara F. to life imprisonment for four accounts of murder. Her subsequent appeal is dismissed.

Her henchman Konrad C. must serve a 12-year prison sentence.

In 2014, Barbara F. sues the new owner of her house, which has since been put up for compulsory auction. She states that he had unlawfully disposed of objects from her personal property. The lawsuit is dismissed.

CHAPTER 14:
Pathological Affection

Since the beginning of their school days, 18-year-old Martin S. and 19-year-old Andreas P. from a town in southern Germany have been the embodiment of very best friends.

As children, they were inseparable on the local playgrounds and in the woods. In school, they sat next to each other and spent every free minute together. And now they attend the commercial high school in a neighbouring town together.

Yet, external appearances are deceptive. From the beginning of their friendship, the two boys from wealthy families have never been on the same level. Andreas P. is much calmer, more reserved and insecure, and so Martin S. leads the way. In the past, he was the only one who decided what they would play and do together. Nothing has changed about that to this day.

Andreas P. continues to look up to his friend, who is a few months younger, and is unable to imagine life without him. Deep down inside, he is firmly convinced that he will never be able to find another or even a better friend. For this reason, he still willingly follows Martin S.'s instructions on his way to adulthood as he did in primary school.

The parents of the two young men are also good acquaintances.

In 2009, Martin S. accepts the invitation of Andreas P.'s parents to dinner on Holy Thursday. During the cosy get-together, the young men talk openly about their future plans.

After dinner, the two friends say goodbye because they want to watch an exciting film which has just been released on DVD at Martin's place

When they arrive at the house of the S. family, Martin's parents, a 57-year-old alternative practitioner and his 55-year-old housewife, have already set off to spend the evening in a pub.

In the living room, Martin S.'s sisters sit in front of the television giggling, with a large bowl of popcorn. One of the two pretty, sometimes a little cocky young women is 22, the other 24 years old. Both recently made the decision to study pedagogy together.

In accordance with their long-established habits, Martin S. and Andreas P. go straight upstairs after a short greeting. But in Martin S.'s room they don't even start to think of a film. Instead they put on the discarded jeans, the dark rain jackets and the rubber shoes waiting for them at the wardrobe floor. From the hiding place behind the dresser, they fetch the small-calibre pistols that the two young men had stolen from the clubhouse of their marksmen's club six months earlier.

Then they descend the stairs, calmly and with a sober mind. Without even thinking about it for a second, Andreas P. points his gun at Martin S's unsuspecting sisters. One of the two young women is hit by ten bullets, the other by nine. They use empty plastic bottles as silencers.

After again changing their clothes shortly afterwards, Martin S. and Andreas P. pay Martin's parents a visit. As if nothing had happened at all, they sit at their table for half an hour in the restaurant where the parents are staying. During the following light-hearted conversation they do not raise any suspicion.

Afterwards they go back home to Martin S., where they change their clothes again. They wait, behind the front door, until Martin's parents return. As soon as they enter the house shortly after midnight, they shoot them at close range without the slightest warning, the father with eight bullets, the mother with three.

As he has done countless times before, Martin S. then stays overnight with his friend Andreas P. Both sleep deeply and firmly.

On Good Friday morning, the two young men return to Martin S.'s house, from where he informs the police at 11:00 AM. With clearly perceptible horror in his voice, he pretends they discovered the bodies of his family on their arrival a few minutes ago.

Since there are no signs of burglary, it does not take long until the suspicions of the arriving investigators falls at the two friends. These behave strangely, but they still deny having anything to do with the crimes.

After the investigators can prove traces of gunpowder on their hands, the judge issues the arrest warrants on Saturday.

Following this, Andreas P. folds during his interrogation. He confesses that they committed the crime together and reveals the hiding places of the clothes and weapons used for the murders.

A total of thirty shots were fired from the weapons. In connection with these devious crimes, Martin S. and Andreas P. are also held responsible for breaking into the clubhouse of the marksmen's club. In October last year, they captured 17 rifles and pistols with 1,700 rounds of ammunition.

At the side-lines of the investigations, additional so far unsolved, smaller burglaries are revealed, which the two friends committed "out of pure adventure desire" in the year 2007. Among other things, they stole a computer and a beamer from a school at that time. In a supermarket, they stole cash, alcohol and cigarettes, although none of them smoked.

The trial against the alleged perpetrators is opened in October 2009 in front of the youth chamber of the regional court. Because of the great public interest in this case, the judges decide to allow some journalists selected in advance to participate in the hearing.

Both perpetrators confess in court. Andreas P. continues to hold fast to his statement that he fired the deadly shots alone. Martin S. would have planned the crime and asked him to carry it out. But he would not have been able to murder his family all by himself.

On the sixth day of the trial, Martin S. confirmed his friend's statement. Only in one point their statements contradict each other. While Andreas P. states that Martin S. had been directly behind him in all four murders, Martin S. insists that he had been in another room.

The psychiatric expert voices the suspicion that Martin S. would have acted out of pure greed in order to have the entire inheritance of around 270,000 Euro all for himself to finally be able to move out of his unloved home. At the same time he wanted to free himself from his father, whom he regarded as a tyrant.

In contrast, the expert assumes that Andreas P. was driven to his deed by his blind, platonic affection for Martin S. This would have given him the hope to further strengthen their friendship and to bind them together for all time.

In the further course of the trial, Andreas P. informs the court that his friend had been increasingly unhappy in his parental home. Above all because of his strict, dominant father, he would have felt permanently misunderstood and isolated. That's why he had been thinking about wiping out his family for a year. He would have come to the conclusion: "There are only two possibilities left. Either my family lives on or me."

The defender of Martin S. confirms the statements of Andreas P. As far as he can judge, his client would have suffered day after day for years under the strict rules, humiliations and prohibitions of his father. For this reason, he ultimately escaped reality into a realm of fantasy in which he killed himself or his family.

However, Martin S. doesn't seem to have grasped the full implications of the consequences of his atrocious deeds. Despite his problematic relationship with his father, which his best friend sees as the decisive trigger for his plan, he confesses to his lawyer in private: "The worst thing is that I miss my father so much now".

Andreas P.'s bewildered parents are absolutely certain that their son did not commit this almost unimaginable crime for material reasons. He would have been dependent on his friend Martin S. in every respect. Only for this reason would he have done everything for his best friend without exception.

At the end of the trial, the court comes to the decision to sentence Martin S. to life imprisonment under adult criminal law with particularly severe guilt.

Following this verdict, a professor for criminal law takes the view that the court violated one of the basic rules by appointing a psychiatric for adults instead of an adolescent psychiatric as the evaluator. However, the Federal Supreme Court cannot find any legal errors and confirms the judgement.

Since Andreas P. suffers from a provable developmental disorder, the court agrees on a conviction under juvenile criminal law in his case. It doesn't matter in any way that he's actually the older one of the two. The court is charging him with a ten-year juvenile sentence.

How the two young men are able to continue living with the memory of their deeds in the future is beyond the jurisdiction of the court.

CHAPTER 15:
Six Mysterious Letters

In October 1984, 34-year-old Hartmut T. had already been living for several months in a permanent fear that was incomprehensible to his personal environment. Again and again he tries to convince his wife that "they" are following him and that they will do something to him very soon.

Some time ago, the food technician lost his job. He's been desperately looking for a new job ever since. What torments him so much is not an existential fear.

Basically, Hartmut T. could consider himself lucky. His marriage is going well all in all and he is the proud father of a healthy and lovable daughter.

His wife is increasingly worried about him. Despite all her efforts, however, she can no longer get through to him. Every day, he seems more absent and scattered.

As almost every evening on 25 October 1984, he sits next to his wife in his comfortable favourite armchair in front of the television. Together they watch a film which they already know, but which they both would like to see again.

Nevertheless, Hartmut T. sees absent-minded and unaware of the film as to his wife's remarks.

Around 11:00 AM he jumps up out of the blue and shouts: "Now I finally get what's going on here. Everyone has conspired against me."

At the same moment he tears off a note from the notepad on the desk at the window and hastily scribbles the six capital letters "YOG'TZE" onto the paper. These do not make up a common word or a recognisable meaning.

A few seconds later he crosses out the letters again.

Shortly afterwards, Hartmut T. says goodbye to his wife, because he is out for a quick drive to the neighbouring village to drink a beer in his local pub.

And exactly that is what he tries to do. After ordering the beer, he suddenly falls off the chair. From this fall some scratches remain in his face.

Later, however, it becomes absolutely clear that Hartmut T. was not drunk. Consequently, there must have been another reason for this embarrassing mishap.

He apologizes to his acquaintances, telling them he had had a short blackout. Before leaving the pub, he drinks a schnapps and a glass of orange juice.

He doesn't hit the road home, however. Instead, he drives through the rural area in the western part of the country to the neighbouring home of his mother and brothers.

About an hour after midnight, when the whole village is asleep, Hartmut T. rings the bell of a 76-year-old neighbour of his mother, whom he knows very well since his childhood. The old lady, considered extraordinarily religious, opens a window and sends the supposedly drunken man home with friendly, calming words. With the gloomy prophecy: "Something terrible will happen this night", he urges her to a talk.

Then the nice neighbour advises him to better get back to his close-by family home, which Hartmut T. declines. He explains that no one would understand him there. Finally, he promises the old lady to take her advice to heart and drive home to his wife.

After he has turned around to dive into the darkness of the night, his trail is lost for about two hours.

Later it turns out that he had no intention of returning home after all. Instead, he drove towards the nearest big city on a main road.

At first sight, Hartmut T. left the road shortly before an exit and landed his car in the ditch.

At this place, two truck drivers discover his completely dented car around 3:00 AM. They immediately stop and walk towards the vehicle to help the occupants who may be in distress.

At the crash site they are confronted with an alarming sight. The severely injured Hartmut T. is sitting in the passenger seat, undressed. His entire body is covered with dirt and leaves. In the footwell of the driver's seat his shoes lie neatly next to each other. The removed ignition key is found later in the rear area of the car on the hat rack.

Since the dying man is still temporarily conscious, with his last strength, he tries to tell the two helpers that there were four more men in the car with him. They supposedly have fled by now.

When asked if they were friends of his, he shakes his head.

Immediately, one of the truck drivers calls the police from an emergency telephone and asks for an ambulance. Despite the efforts of the emergency doctors, Hartmut T. dies on his way to the hospital.

During their interrogation, the truck drivers independently testify they had seen a blond man in a light jacket with blood stains on his sleeve near the scene of the accident from their vehicle. The man would have walked around Hartmut T.'s car, but was no longer there when they arrived.

In the course of the subsequent investigations, it turns out that Hartmut T. has not suffered the serious injuries in his car. According to the findings of the investigation, Hartmut T. was run over by an unknown car in another place on the night of his death and was only then put in the passenger seat of his car. He was already undressed when he was run over. Only the damage to his vehicle originates from the place where his car was found.

The officials are faced with a mystery with numerous baffling details. Without the slightest doubt, Hartmut T. was almost suffering panic-stricken fear during the last hours of his life. But of what?

In one of the final interviews, Hartmut T.'s wife only

half a year later remembers the mysterious six letters her husband had scribbled on a piece of paper. What could YOG'TZE mean?

His wife claims to have carelessly thrown away the note before the news of her husband's death. Did this note with the mysterious sequence of letters actually exist?

Only one thing is certain. The sequence of letters that Hartmut T.'s wife has memorized does not make any sense. If it was supposed to be a word, it does not exist in any language of this world.

In a well-known television programme, the public is informed about the mysterious case and the strange letters and asked for relevant information. Thereupon, several amateur radio operators come forward and propose in accordance to replace one of the letters by a number similar to it. This would result in a Romanian radio signal. But even this realization does not take the investigators a single step further.

Another spectator mentions a hitchhiker looking for a lift near the scene of the accident during the night in question. Immediately the police ask this stranger to report. He hasn't done that to this date.

Indications that Hartmut T. had established contacts with the local drug scene in the Netherlands during his holidays soon fizzle out as well.

Although a reward of 3,000 DM waits and more than 170 calls are received from all over Germany and from neighbouring countries after the television programme, not a single piece of information leads to a useful result.

To this day, the events leading to the death of Hartmut T. cannot be reconstructed. As far as this crime is concerned, the answers to all those unanswered questions remain hidden in the dark.

For this reason, the puzzle of Hartmut T.'s last night on earth gained the notoriety being one of the most baffling unexplained deaths in German criminal history.

Since murder in this country is not statute-barred, however, the files on crimes like this are not closed and regularly retrieved from the archives. In some of these cases, the latest investigative methods have already produced results.

In order to be able to uncover the secrets of Hartmut T.'s death one day, investigators are relying above all on the current possibilities of DNA analysis.

Useable traces that have been secured on the body of the victim, on the clothes of the dead person and inside his car are still available for this purpose.

After Hartmut T. got run over, he must have been put in his car by a stranger. There's a good chance he left his DNA behind.

So, if the perpetrator is already on file, a DNA comparison could, with a little luck, provide the crucial clue even after such a long time.

Consequently, the hope remains that the murderer of Hartmut K. can still be identified and brought to justice after 35 years.

Closing Remarks by the Author

Dear reader,

Thank you so much for taking the time to read my first book. Even though it is far from perfect, I hope it has touched you as much as it has touched me writing it. Let us all go through the world with eyes attentive for the needs of others and hopefully prevent many more tragedies.

My desire is to write about further cases from beyond the German borders. With a positive rating on Amazon you can help me. For criticism, ideas, feedback and inspiration I am grateful, you can contact me in writing at the following e-mail address. AdrianLangenscheid(at)mail.de

Your Adrian Langenscheid

Follow me on:
Instagram: @true_crime_international

Facebook:
https://www.facebook.com/True-Crime-Deutschland-Adrian-Langenscheid

www.ingramcontent.com/pod-product-compliance
Lightning Source LLC
Chambersburg PA
CBHW031311060726
47590CB00003B/1151